LETTERS FROM CONGO

Other titles from Central Square Press

A HARD SUMMATION by Afaa Michael Weaver

CRACKED CALABASH by Lisa Pegram

THE NEXT VERSE POETS MIXTAPE - VOLUME ONE: The 4 x 4
by Melanie Henderson, Fred Joiner, Lisa Pegram, Enzo Silon Surin

FEAR OF DOGS & OTHER ANIMALS by Shauna M. Morgan

A LETTER OF RESIGNATION: AN AMERICAN LIBRETTO
by Enzo Silon Surin

LETTERS FROM CONGO

poems

Danielle Legros Georges

CENTRAL SQUARE PRESS

All inquiries and permissions requests should be addressed to the Publisher:

Central Square Press
Lynn, Massachusetts

publisher@centralsquarepress.com
www.centralsquarepress.com

Printed in the United States of America
First Edition

ISBN-13: 978-1-941604-05-2

ISBN-10: 1-941604-05-6

Grateful acknowledgment is made to the editors of *Jalada/Transition* in which the following poems first appeared: "Instructions in Times of Emergency," "The Lake behind You" and "Makak":

Cover art: Map of Zaire (West Central Region) U.S. Army Map Service 1:2,000,000 1957, revised 1961. Courtesy of the University of Texas Libraries, the University of Texas at Austin.

Book design: Enzo Silon Surin

dedicated to Thérèse and Edouard Legros
moun mwen

CONTENTS

letters from congo

Instructions in Times of Emergency

Keep the radio low but listen.
A slow rustle. (A dictator.)

To survive do not turn
(though some turn)

against a neighbor.
Refrain from looking

a beached and bloated
body in its face. Don't

plead to God. Witness
the executions. Your human

self, keep it alive. A type
of flame. The prisons—full.

Your lizard self.
Your toughest skin.

Shut your doors tight
against the night. Keep

your doors shut
against the creeping

night. It crawls
on all fours. The morning

will not come.

The Lake behind You

for my father

In the far-off, the fronds you peer
from paint the photograph green

knee-deep these ferns, a jungle's
monuments, trees grown equatorial

a *hot hell* you call it.
Aeropost blue.

Your letter arrives. Your mother
opens it. And since your demise

I open it again.

————

New world man returned
to source: *Africain.*

If there can be such a thing
as clean back to origin.

In Port-au-Prince your name
snaked down a list. *Good riddance*

hummed Duvalier. His palace
balcony. His balustrades.

When they called your name

you said *yes, I'm going*
and you went. You went.

———

The Inongo sky is a milky blue.
The lake behind you is full of crocodiles.

Dear Brother

I Pray That The United Nations Bureau Will Forward
This Card To My Brother Rodney Georges Who Is
Currently In The Congo, Whose Address I Don't Know

———

Fischbach, Germany
1 February 1966

Dear Brother,

Our mother made me aware that you have been in the Congo
since the month of October 1965. She complains of no word
from you. I'm sure all is well. What kind of work are you doing?

Already 7 years since we separated. Time has stopped for me.
I don't age. I'm taken for 23 despite being 33. I'm working
as an engineer at Dornier. Here the first vertical transport plane

is being built. It has 10 reaction motors. I'm the only foreigner,
not to mention the only black man in this company. I earn a good
living. I bought a big Citroen ID19. I'll send photos soon. Send me

your address. I hope this card reaches you. Good luck and happy
new year to you and your family. Write me soon.

Your brother, Gerard

Letter from Léo

Léopoldville
17 February1966

Dear Daco,

I imagine how much you've suffered, with no news from me for three months. I suffered because of this. I went—rather, was sent—to a horrible place, a real hell. Not only generally

hostile, but the local authorities, who don't like Haitians, did all they could to discourage us. When we asked them in December to put us in touch with our employer, the central government

—they cut all communication with the exterior. Our letters were blocked at the provincial post office. We were, in effect, prisoners.

Fortunately, I left this cursed province. The central government is looking into this all, but we were in the right. If everything works out I'll stay in Léo or go to a more welcoming city.

Dear mother, the bank of Canada hasn't yet updated me on my account. I can send you nothing. Not sure if the bank received my transfer in dollars. I must send a sample signature so that everything can be straightened out.

If Léo gives us trouble, I'll leave the country and go to Germany to see Gerard and look for work, and study. If this doesn't work, I'll go myself to the UNITED STATES, and in case this doesn't work, I'll return to Haiti.

What's important for me right now is to have Gerard's address in Germany. If you can send it by cable as soon as possible I'd be happy. I wrote to Serge, you, and Edouard, each of you two letters from INONGO. They were, no doubt, confiscated at INONGO.

Now I am at the address above. While waiting for your news receive dear mother the affection and kisses of your son Rodney who has never stopped thinking of you.

N.B. Let me know too by letter Roger's address in the U.S. I will write you soon.

Rodney   Say hello to everyone for me

Mother Chérie

BP 5208 / LEO 10 / Léopoldville/ Congo
23 March 196z236

Mother Chérie,

I received your lovely letter. It was a great comfort to me.
Thank you for Gerard's address. I wrote him 10 days ago.
He hasn't yet written back.

You surely received the $50 from the Bank of Canada.
I sent it to you almost a month ago.

I am doing well enough, but I'm worried. Since arriving
at Léo I've sent Edmonde 4 letters plus $600 but have no
word from her. She told me she was planning to go to
Port-au-Prince to wait for her ticket. Did she do this?

I'm still awaiting the decision of the authorities of Léo.
I'm at the point of being re-assigned. I don't know where.

Say hello to Yanme, Gladys, Maxime for me.

Your son Rodney who loves you very much.

Headwaters

for my mother

three infants in tow

a plane   an address

in hand   a husband

in a distant   place

how long   how far

how streams

of air

what is ahead   and what

behind   what   after

the books hidden

the mouths sealed

the alarmed

tributaries

———

a leaf dropped

in headwaters

of the Congo River

bobs up and down

thousands of kilometers

past rapids   past vast

waterfalls

on slow

currents

to meet the Atlantic Ocean

Your Grown- and Grand-Children

Tschikapa
6 March 1967

Dear Mother Daco,

It's been a long time since I have written. I see that you're worried but there's been nothing terrible, just some negligence on my part. We spent the year-end break in Luluabourg, another town.

I set up house when we got back, decorating the children's room, making small colored blankets for their beds. That took some time.

I received your New Year's card, and the childrens' card too. They're well, so is Rodney, who will write you. Summer's coming soon, and we'll have to move. Rodney will tell you that our vacation plans have changed. Instead of to Jamaica, we're going to Puerto Rico, where things are less expensive. Don't pack too many dresses for the trip, you'll find some at good prices there.

Laurette wrote me to tell me how much you've spoiled her and her children. If she can help you when you leave the country, you can always speak to her.

I'm sending you a small photo, which isn't very beautiful but in which you'll find your grown and your grand children.

Edmonde

Everyone sends you kisses

Beer and Babies

There is no television. It's hot. What else
is there to do? Hell!

The men are making new lives here.
Us? We're growing new lives.

What's cooking? The Belgians. The Congolese.

We crossed an ocean. A world on fire.

Ask us, we'll tell you.

We're making new lives.

New towns. New rivers. New cities.

The new huge city.

New dictator. Same dictator.

Same invisible hands.

Same invisible hands.

Sisters who are our sisters.

Beer for the afternoons.

New children.

Born here.

Makak

The men are called *boys*, and the women *mamas*
in the houses of the colony's masters
on the land of the boys and mamas.

The whites are called masters and the natives
makaks, and even with each other
they say *makak*.

And we say makak too at the smallest infraction,
at the least mistake in the land of the boys
and the mamas.

The men enter the white houses to cook
and clean, the women to watch
the babies by day.

The mambas glide through impossible grasses,
climb up the tallest trees. The makaks
are themselves,

not knowing they're insults. They move swiftly
from tree to tree. They screech
in the night.

Of makaks and mamas and masters and boys
we can say this: A makak and *boy*
will become a man who becomes

a leopard who plays master, then is master
and the houses burn, and the fields
blow to ashes.

And the ashes, they whisper *makak*.

**Letter to our Parents We Do not Know We are Writing
(from Aunt Laurette's House, Port-au-Prince)**

Return, though we are well fed and schooled
Return, powdered with love
Return, though precariously
Return, though our passel of cousins love us
Return, though we love them
Return with mother's milk and father's milk
Return as the day turns clear, the afternoon rains over
The clouds like ships
The red school uniforms
Return with books from abroad
With *feux d'artifice*, stars so close to the earth in the night's blue smoke
Return with the pink meat of almonds
With the butter of dawn
With the morning mail

Boy God, Junk Pile

Who does not love Tintin, boy reporter, not knowing
I too am the native coming with the saw to saw off

the tail of Milou, the talking dog, en route to the Congo.
Who dives into the water off the ship on those watercolor

pages. The jade-blue. Next. I am in the crowd of natives,
the one wearing a boot and a shoe by the rickety railroad.

To greet the great Tintin. A boy. A god. I am Tintin boy
god. Who takes on the roaring lion, who takes on a tribe

of Africans, who vanquishes the evil medicine man.
Returning triumphant. Pith helmet. Uniform of khakis.

The pages almost turn themselves. Quick. What is
the frame? Tintin, boy reporter on assignment. What is

the lesson? Is the lesson in Creole where *tintin* means junk?
The Creole *tintin* has no youth to offer the Belgian

tale. It's just *old junk*. As in "he went to that girl's
house and did some tintin in front of her family. Imagine

that!" As in "That tintin tried to play me." As in "What
tintin are you telling me now?"

Edmonde en Route to Matadi

Brussels
14 January 1968

Hello Mother Daco,

I am writing you from Brussels where I spent the day.
I've had a good trip so far. Luckily I have my very warm
coat. Already in New York there was an intense cold.
At the Brussels airport, it was even worse. We walked
in snow.

I'm thinking so much of the children today, but I know
they're well. I resigned myself to leaving without them,
it's for their well being—with all my small ones here,
Rodney would be the only one working.

Tomorrow night I will be in the Congo and Tuesday
with Rodney in Matadi.

Take care.

Go often to see the children, and give me news of them.
I will write more lengthily in the Congo.

Kisses,

Edmonde

Postcard |Front and Back

A tall tree, what type I do not know. Standing in a vast grassland. Swollen clouds across an expanse of sky. The palest horizon. An antelope herd, unsurprised and grazing. A picture-taker far and stiller than the faunae: long legs on large hooves. Frozen in their antelope business. The tree is humming. The clouds moving forever nowhere.

———————

Kinshasa
4 January 1969

Dear Mother Daco,

I could not write you before because it's been 4 months since I've been paid. Things are going better now. We're working to establish ourselves in the U.S.A. You'll be with us in August.

I am wishing you, along with Edmonde, a good and happy '69.

Good health,

à bientôt,

Roro

Everyone is doing well. Send me information on whether one can change one's passport in Haiti. Mine has been cancelled.

Notes

Between 1960 and 1975, hundreds of young Haitian professionals moved to and worked in the Congo (later to be Zaire, and the Democratic Republic of the Congo). With little opportunity to practice in their fields, and with many facing persecution under the Duvalier regime, most saw the recruitment of Francophone educators by the new Congolese government and the United Nations Educational, Scientific and Cultural Organization (UNESCO) as a way to escape repression in Haiti, start new lives in Africa, and participate in a decolonizing Congo. My parents were among them.

Rodney Georges	my father
Edmonde Legros Georges	my mother
Daco (Ilda St. Jean)	my father's mother
Gerard Georges	my father's brother
Laurette Legros Dorcé	my mother's sister

———————————

Instructions in Times of Emergency
Addresses the pervasive fear and persecution experienced under the Duvalier dictatorship (beginning in 1957) which forced many Haitians to emigrate.

23

The Lake behind You
Inongo, a town in the western part of the Democratic Republic of the Congo (DRC).

Letter from Léo
Léopoldville, Léo for short, the Belgian colonial name for the capital of the DRC. Léopoldville was renamed Kinshasa in 1966.

Headwaters
Language for second half of poem is drawn and amended from www.wwf-congobasin.org.

Makak
Haitian Creole for monkey. Also phonetic spelling of French word *macaque*, monkey.

Letter to our Parents We Do not Know We are Writing (from Aunt Laurette's House, Port-au-Prince)
feux d'artifice, French for fireworks.

Boy God, Junk Pile
References the children's book *Tintin Au Congo*, part of the popular Francophone *Les Aventures de Tintin* series of comic books written by Georges Remi under the pen name Hergé.

Edmonde en Route to Matadi
Brussels, the capital of Belgium. Matadi, a port city in the far western part of the DRC.

about the author

Danielle Legros Georges is a poet, essayist, translator, and professor in the Creative Arts in Learning Division of Lesley University. She curates Boston-based and international poetry events, and is the author of two books of poems, *Maroon* and *The Dear Remote Nearness of You*, and editor of *City of Notions: An Anthology of Contemporary Boston Poems.* In 2014 she was appointed Boston's Poet Laureate.

CPSIA information can be obtained
at www.ICGtesting.com
Printed in the USA
BVOW09s1534230917
495682BV00001B/9/P